IMAGES
of America

AROUND
NEW FREEDOM

IMAGES
of America

AROUND
NEW FREEDOM

Bob Ketenheim

ARCADIA
PUBLISHING

Published by Arcadia Publishing
Charleston, South Carolina

Library of Congress Catalog Card Number: 2005924553

For all general information contact Arcadia Publishing at:
Telephone 843-853-2070
Fax 843-853-0044
E-mail sales@arcadiapublishing.com
For customer service and orders:
Toll-Free 1-888-313-2665

Visit us on the Internet at www.arcadiapublishing.com

To Vera McCullough,
a lifelong resident of New Freedom and a devoted servant of God.

CONTENTS

ACKNOWLEDGMENTS

I am grateful to the following people who unselfishly shared their documents, their memories, their photographs, and, most importantly, their time: Fae Adams, Phil Attig, Dick Baade, Hazel Berholdt, Jim Boddington, Miriam Bradfield, Shirley Carbaugh, Ruth and Lamar Carman, Bill and Dianne Donahue, Sabilla Ernst, Chris and Leah Geary, Roland Gemmill, Jean Glatfelter, Marge Goodfellow, David Helfrich, Corenthia Henry, Bob and Jean Hittie, Erin Holloway, Rev. Mark and Mary Hopkins, Ed and Kay Hughes, Mayor Jeff Joy, Joe and Sandy Koller, Daniel Jesse Mays, Kerry and Deb McKnight, Sue Myers, Joanne and Richard Nace, Neal Panzarella, Shelley Pokrivka, Brenda Putnam, Mary and Bill Reed, Jim Reynolds, Doug and Lee Ann Shope, Wilfred Shuchart, Virginia Smith, Mike and Jackie Summers, Tom and Jane Summers, Don Tesno, Anna Mae and Clifton Wineholt, Louise Winter, Nancy Wirtz, Joan Yohe, and Bernard "Nardie" Young.

A special thank-you is extended to Melissa Stewart and the staff of the Southern York County Library for their assistance and cooperation; the members of the New Freedom Heritage for their dedication to preserving New Freedom's history; and Vera McCullough for her hard work in seeing this project through. She arranged interviews, tracked down photographs and information, and made phone calls, all while running her business.

And a thank-you goes to my wife, Patti, and daughters, Erin and Katie, for their support and their patience.

INTRODUCTION

The intent of this book is not to tell the history of New Freedom and its surrounding area. The intent is merely to show how certain things used to look. For those interested in the rich history of New Freedom, please refer to the New Freedom centennial book. Although copies are hard to find nowadays, the Southern York County Library has several copies. The library also has numerous other books, articles, and photographs that provide a glimpse of New Freedom's good old days.

Shrewsbury Township, in which New Freedom is situated, was one of the first Pennsylvania settlements west of the Susquehanna River. It was established by an act of the Pennsylvania General Assembly in 1739. The township originally included all the land that is now occupied by Hopewell, Shrewsbury, and Springfield Townships. In 1749, York County was formed and the city of York was established as its county seat.

The land in the southern part of York County was found to be fertile and available for farming. It attracted many settlers who were looking for a new beginning. Conrad W. Free, known as the "Founding Father of New Freedom," settled here in 1783. He and his wife, Maria, had eight children. One of their sons, Peter Free, moved his family to the area from Baltimore County, Maryland, in 1823 and built a log cabin in the area that is now South Third Street.

Peter Free and his wife, Naomi, had 13 children—seven boys and six girls. Four of the boys—John, Eli, Adam, and Jared—became physicians. Dr. John Free practiced medicine in Dillsburg, New Freedom, and Stewartstown. Dr. Eli Free practiced in New Freedom from 1860 to 1890. He then moved to Baltimore and continued his medical practice until his death. Dr. Adam Free practiced in New Freedom before moving to Harrisburg. Dr. Jared Free entered the U.S. Army as a surgeon. He was killed in action in Virginia during the Civil War. His grave, as well as many others of the Free family, is in the Rock Chapel Cemetery in southern Shrewsbury Township. Although descendants of Conrad Free live today, none are known to be in New Freedom.

In August 1838, the Baltimore and Susquehanna Railroad had completed its line south from York to the Maryland state line. Seventeen years later, a four-railroad merger resulted in the North Central Railroad. The North Central built a railway station in New Freedom in 1859–1860 to provide a shipping and receiving terminal.

New Freedom was incorporated in 1873. Freedom was the first name picked for the town; however, another small town in western Pennsylvania already had that name. Not to be discouraged, the people finally settled on New Freedom.

The railroad had a major impact on New Freedom's agricultural and industrial development. It provided an efficient means to bring in raw materials and to transport out farm-harvested and factory-finished products. In 1900, a wire cloth factory was built on the east side of the main-line tracks. When the wire cloth business moved out of town in 1916, the American Insulator Company (AICO) moved into the factory. Over the years, the company expanded its factory facilities several times. By the time the company went out of business in 1986, it had provided employment for thousands of local residents.

The canning business was a large New Freedom employer for over 75 years. J. P. Hoffacker operated the first canning factory in town. J. P. Colgan built a large cannery along High Street. George Ruhl and William H. Freed later operated that cannery before it was purchased by Charles G. Summers Jr. Inc.

The sewing industry was another large employer in New Freedom. Several small sewing shops and factories were located in various buildings around the borough. Louis Zupnick Inc., the M&R Garment Company, and York County Sewing Company were still in business into the 1970s.

The railroad also provided employment for scores of area residents. Engineers, brakemen, conductors, repairmen, dispatchers, track workers, and telegraphers were among the local residents who made their living on the rails. By the time of the railroad's demise, New Freedom had grown deep roots as a peaceful and prosperous residential community for hundreds of people who worked in Baltimore, Harrisburg, Washington, D.C., and York.

New Freedom celebrated its centennial in 1973. The importance of the railroad in New Freedom's growth and development is apparent by looking at the town's official centennial seal. The seal contains the caricatures of not one but two steam locomotives prominently displayed around its center.

One

THE RAILROAD

As cities and towns along the Mississippi River owe their existence and growth to the river, New Freedom owes much of what it is today to the railroad. Before there was New Freedom, there was the railroad through the area. The original line that ran through what would become New Freedom was the Baltimore and Susquehanna Railroad. In January 1855, the Baltimore and Susquehanna merged with three other railroads to form the North Central Railroad. In 1874, the Pennsylvania Railroad took control of the North Central Railroad.

The New Freedom station was built from 1859 to 1860. In the bay window section of the station was a telegraph office. The station operated from 5:00 a.m. to 9:00 p.m., when the last train passed through. The station was in continuous service for freight and passengers until it closed in 1965. Scheduled passenger train service stopped running through the area in 1969.

Before high-speed highways, nearly everyone traveled the rails. Passenger trains brought shoppers and businessmen into town. The businessmen would stay at local hotels while they peddled their wares to shopkeepers and residents. During the Civil War, World War I, and especially World War II, troop trains were a common sight.

This 1920s view of the station shows the heavy carts that were used to load freight and baggage onto the trains. From here, farmers shipped milk daily and eggs, butter, chickens, and produce weekly. Peoples Baking Company shipped fresh baked goods daily. In the spring, shipments of fresh fish would arrive from towns along the Susquehanna River. Cattle and coal were other important commodities that arrived by rail.

In June 1972, Tropical Storm Agnes moved north through the area, and the resulting heavy rains and swollen stream and creek beds washed out many of the railroad's bridges, culverts, and underpasses. Those north of the Mason-Dixon were repaired, but those in Maryland were not. Rail service between York and Baltimore had come to an end. Over the years, the abandoned freight station fell into disrepair.

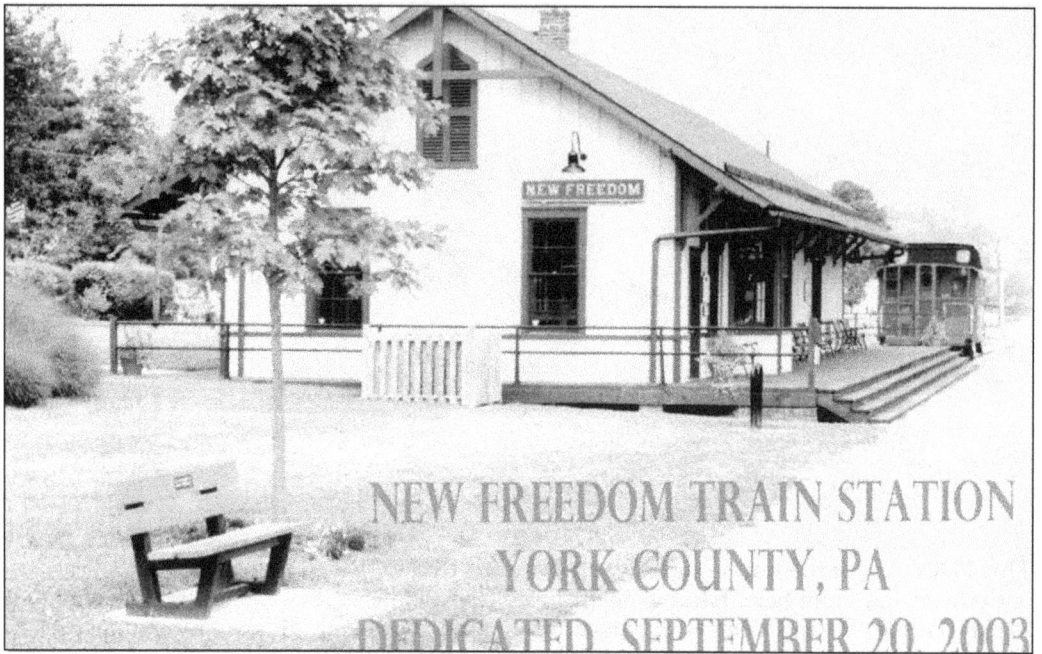

NEW FREEDOM TRAIN STATION
YORK COUNTY, PA
DEDICATED SEPTEMBER 20, 2003

In the 1990s, local citizens began the arduous task of rebuilding and preserving the old freight station. The station was completely dismantled, the wood was cleaned and preserved, and the building was reassembled using as much of the original materials as possible. The rebuilt station was dedicated on September 20, 2003, and it now houses a small restaurant and a museum that celebrates New Freedom history.

On the left is the feed mill built by Milton W. Bahn in 1872. It later became the Farmers' Exchange and Summit Service. The two-family house on the left was occupied by William Miller family and the Thomas McCullough family. The house was last used as a York County Sewing Company factory. Crescent Industries now occupies the land. On the right is the Marble and Granite Cemetery Memorial building, which W. C. Meads built and H. N. Bailey later owned. In the distance on the right beyond the department store are the wire cloth factory and the Stewartstown Railroad station. The Stewartstown Railroad interlined with the Pennsylvania Railroad at New Freedom in 1885.

12

On the left of this southward view are the buildings and the smokestack of the New Freedom Wire Cloth Factory (later the American Insulator Company). In the distance on the left is Spector's Department Store. The Mays Building has not yet been built, which dates this picture before 1909. The train station can be seen on the right just beyond the oil tank. The railroad was obviously prospering as six sets of tracks can be seen.

Because New Freedom sits at the top of a grade, some longer and heavier trains required the assistance of helper or pusher locomotives. This is a picture of one such helper locomotive that was stationed in the area. These locomotives and the local engineers who operated them were on call 24 hours a day, 7 days a week. When a train was unable to make the grade, a runner was sent to the engineer's home to wake him to man his steam engine. The engines were kept on a siding on the north end of town until needed. Once diesel locomotives began running the line, helper engines were no longer needed.

Maurice McDonald stands in front of a trackside oil house in 1920. The oil house stood on the north side of the New Freedom rail yard across from the Costa farm. The building housed the equipment and oil that were necessary to maintain the helper engines.

On the south end of New Freedom stood the Flickerville tower, otherwise known as NF. It was located near the tracks on South Front Street. From this building, railroad employees controlled signals and dispatched trains. It was also the location of one of the railroad telegraph offices. As more modern automatic signals were developed, the tower was no longer needed. It was abandoned in 1932 and razed a few years later. The last telegrapher at the tower was Roland F. Baughman.

This snow-packed steam locomotive shows signs of some of the difficulties of early rail transportation. The southbound locomotive is seen in the New Freedom yard. The train is very similar to that of the pay train that stopped to pay railroad employees in New Freedom. The date of this photograph is unknown, so it is unclear if the building in the background then was operated by New Freedom Wire Cloth or the American Insulator Company, which took over the facility in 1916.

This passenger train passes under the Singer Road Bridge. The bridge, shown here under construction, linked the Ryer and Bailey farms on the southern end of town. A replacement bridge is at this location today. The Bailey farm is now one of the many housing developments on the south side of New Freedom.

When the railroad was thriving in the area, railroad employees would receive their pay from clerks who rode a special pay train. This picture shows one of those special trains stopped near the Flickerville tower on the south end of New Freedom.

In the days before automatic grade-crossing signals, watchmen who were employed by the railroad alerted drivers to the approach of a train. Such was the case where Main Street crossed the railroad. Pictured here is Otis Swam. He was the last railroad watchman to guard the highway-railroad crossing in New Freedom.

After the demise of rail service through New Freedom, and before the opening of the Heritage Trail, rail enthusiasts found another way to utilize the rails. These small gasoline-powered maintenance-of-way cars and track-inspection cars were a common sight on weekends in New Freedom. Enthusiasts would spend hours riding north and south along the tracks.

An effort was made in the 1990s to use the existing rails to operate a successful dinner train that ran between New Freedom and York. Unfortunately, the venture did not succeed, and the track again lay dormant. Except for a few cabooses that still stand nearby on the tracks, little remains of the rail service that ensured New Freedom's early growth and survival.

Two

CHURCHES AND SCHOOLS

The first Catholic church was a log-cabin-style structure built in 1842 on the east side of North Constitution Avenue on land donated to the church by Meinard Muller. The church was dedicated by the Right Reverend Gabriel Rempler. It served as place of worship for 63 years. This structure stood close to the site of the red-brick church that replaced it. Fr. John Neumann, later canonized by the Pope, served in New Freedom in 1841, before the log church was built.

In 1905, the log cabin church was replaced by a red-brick structure that still stands on the east side of North Constitution Avenue. This church served the Roman Catholic parish until it was replaced in 1989 by the new church at the top of the hill behind this building. The church on North Constitution Avenue is now used for weddings and special ceremonies.

St. Paul's Evangelical Church, built in 1871, stood on the northwest corner of East Main Street and Shrewsbury Avenue (now North Constitution Avenue). The house to the left was the church parsonage. By the early 1930s, services at the church had been discontinued, and both the church and the parsonage were sold in 1934. The church was torn down in the summer of 1934. Since that time, North Constitution Avenue has been widened, taking some of the ground on which the church stood. The parsonage still stands and it is now a private residence.

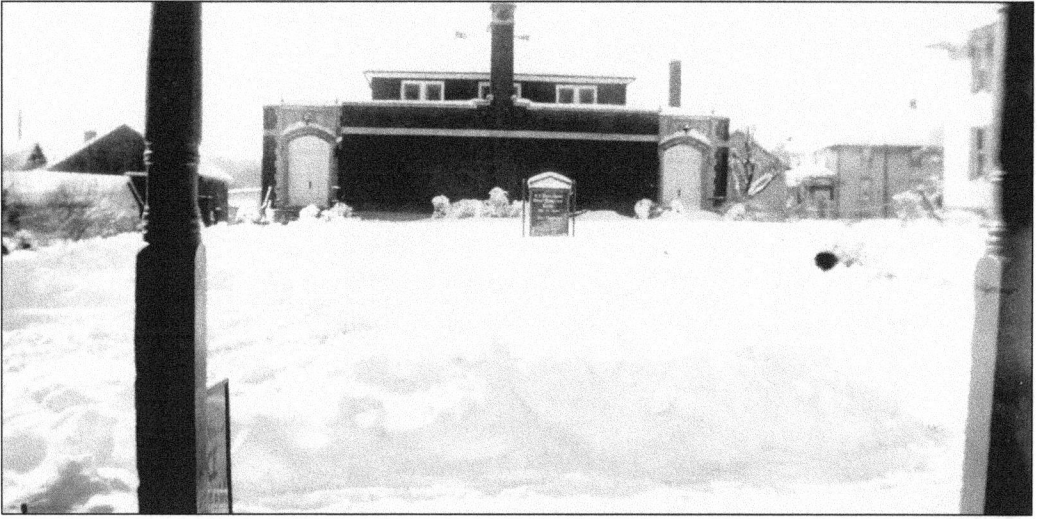

The original Lutheran church was located at 8 West Main Street. When the congregation decided in 1959 to relocate to its present location at 175 East Main Street, the older structure was sold to the local Eastern Star-Triangle Chapter. Since that time, the old church has been used by other congregations as a place of worship and was an exercise facility.

The Methodist congregation began services in a small structure near the Rock Chapel Cemetery south on the trail across from the Shrewsbury Family Restaurant. The original structure of the present-day Methodist church at the intersection of West Franklin and North Second Streets was built in 1871. The sanctuary was added in 1905, and the education building was added in the 1970s.

The Bethany Reformed Church was built in 1860 at 8 North Third Street. In 1884, the church was sold to the Bethany German Reformed Church. Worship services were held here until 1970. The building was eventually sold to the New Freedom Jaycees. It is now Always Better Care, an assisted-living center for the elderly.

The New Freedom Baptist Church was organized in 1947. For the next five years, the congregation worshiped at the New Freedom Community Center on East Main Street. In 1952, the church dedicated its new chapel at 222 North Constitution Avenue. By 1970, the congregation had grown to the point that a larger church was needed. A massive expansion project resulted in the larger place of worship that exists at the same location today.

The origins of Summit Grove Camp go back to Methodist camp meetings that were held along the Susquehanna Trail close to Rock Chapel, which was in the vicinity of the present-day Shrewsbury Family Restaurant. In 1872, the meetings were moved to the grove of trees west of the railroad tracks on the south end of New Freedom. Once established in New Freedom, the camp continued to operate as a Methodist camp until it was acquired by the Christian Missionary Alliance church in 1936.

The Tabernacle is the focal point of the campground. Starting in 1936, the Christian Missionary Alliance Church expanded the site by building dormitories, additional cottages, more camping area, and a swimming pool. The campground's plans to celebrate its centennial in 1972 were dampened by Tropical Storm Agnes. The celebration was held in 1973, the same year that New Freedom celebrated its centennial.

24

In the early 1900s, the number of passengers coming to Summit Grove had increased to the point that a special depot was built on the south end of New Freedom to accommodate them. As many as 10,000 people would congregate there for Sunday worship. Special trains, one from York and two from Baltimore, would bring worshipers to the camp. Also, a solid stream of townspeople walked and rode from downtown New Freedom to the camp. The view above is from 1910, and the view below is from 1914, after the entrance arch had been constructed.

By the time that the Christian Missionary Alliance Church purchased the campground in 1936, many of the buildings were in disrepair, and several had been either heavily damaged or destroyed by fires. In the subsequent years, the remaining buildings were remodeled; an office building, a bookstore, a lunch facility, and three 20-room dormitories were built. The Tabernacle was expanded to seat 1,500 people, and a concrete floor was installed.

Located west of New Freedom on Bowser School Road, this wooden structure burned down and was replaced by a brick structure in the 1920s. Classes were held in this school until 1950. The brick school was one of 13 small schoolhouses in Shrewsbury Township. Eleven of the schoolhouses exist today, mostly as converted residences. The man in the wagon is Benjamin Bowser.

The original New Freedom school, built in the 1830s, was a one-room structure near the site of this structure. It was replaced by a two-room building in 1882. As the town grew, more rooms were added. At times, the overflow of students resulted in classes being held on the second floor of Bailey's Restaurant on East Main Street, on the second floor of Peoples Baking Company at 10 West Main Street, and at the Knights of Pythias Hall.

27

Some students and their teacher at the New Freedom Elementary School pose for this picture in 1895. From left to right, they are as follows: (first row) Curvin Jones, William Bailey, Francis Ryer, Valentine Beikirk, and Arthur Welcome; (second row) Lulu Hershey, Nora Routson, Victoria Ryer, Queenie Reehling, Myra Reehling, Alva Reehling, Viene Newcomer, Dolsie McCullough, and Irene Baughman; (third row) Walter Richie, Grace Miller Mays, Mabel Foust, Grace Mays Ziegler, Julia Beikirk, Sarah Newcomer, Addie Gore, Annie Gillian, and Willie Wilhelm; (fourth row) George Wilhelm, Arthur Nonemaker, Vernon Orwig, Carroll Hederick, unidentified, Emmis Diffenderfer, Mae Foust, and unidentified; (fifth row) Lola Sechrist (teacher), unidentified, Howard Miller, Fred Hartenstein, Alice Nonemaker, Bernard Miller, Erwin Alderson, Bentz Harris, and George Newcomer.

The first class to graduate from New Freedom High School was the class of 1908. The students seated in the front row are, from left to right, Mary Hartenstein Grove, Flo Shirey Rehmeyer, Christiana Besser Rohrbaugh, Grace Standiford, Ethel Taylor, Elizabeth Keener, and Ernest Zeigler.

A New Freedom elementary class is pictured here *c.* 1900. From left to right, they are as follows: (first row) Belva Reehling, William Bailey, Mary Hartenstein, Cora McCullough, Marie Lambert, Grace Miller Mays, Alva Reehling, Queenie Reehling, Margaret Orwig, Dolsie McCullough, and Mary Henry (teacher); (second row) Bernard Miller, Fred Hartenstein, Barnes Kinsing, Addie Gore, Edith Bailey, Myra Reehling, Nellie Grove, and Grace Mays Zeigler; (third row) unidentified, Clifford Koller, Francis Ryer, Valentine Beikirk, Martin Grove, Royston Cuddy, and Ernie Zeigler.

By 1923, the demand for more space was so great that a second floor was added to the school. The upper addition provided two large rooms divided by folding doors that could be opened for student assemblies. Another section had to be added to both levels in 1928. High school and junior high school students attended the New Freedom school until 1951. Sixth grade was moved out of the building in 1968, and grades one through five vacated the building in 1973 upon completion of Southern Elementary. This 1924 view shows the school right after addition of the second floor.

Pictured here is the New Freedom High School class of 1927. Students, from left to right, are as follows: (first row) Martha Walker, Grace Seibel, Beulah Taylor, Pearl Rehmeyer, Florence Gale, and Barbara Ilgenfritz; (second row) Victor Blouse, Emory Grove, Lee Smith, Carroll Sweitzer, Harry Nonemaker, Kenneth Rohrbaugh, and Norman Diehl.

The 1929 New Freedom High School football team is seen here. From left to right are the following: (first row) Stewart C. Bowers Jr., Jacob Hartenstein, Clifton Norris, John Huston, Herman Sellers, Joseph Harvey, and Reed Warner; (second row) Alvin Goodman, Carroll Hunt, Earl Harsher, Paul Smith, Herbert Shaver, Harold Bond, and James Trout.

The 1939 New Freedom High School junior varsity football team is pictured here. From left to right are the following: (first row) Russell Kurtz, Donald Rosier, Arthur Zellers, Robert Franklin, Francis Ziegler, Glenn Young, and Charles Goodfellow; (second row) Jesse Mays, Tyrus Young, Kenneth Bailey, and Franklin Dunnick.

After the New Freedom School finally closed in 1973, the building became the New Freedom Community Center, which was dedicated on August 14, 1976. The large structure on the south side of the building was added as a function hall. The community center continues to provide a place for the New Freedom Business Show, a local office for Help for Oncology Problems and Emotional Support (HOPE), the Lions Club, dances, wedding receptions, a senior center, exercise classes, and other civic functions. In the 1980s, the New Freedom German Fest was held in the hall.

In 1974, the New Freedom Baptist Church built the New Freedom Christian High School on land owned by the church on New Freedom Road (now Campbell Road). The church also has elementary classes at its worship facilities on North Constitution Avenue. The New Freedom Christian High School curriculum focuses on spiritual, academic, and patriotic values.

Three

BUSINESSES

This view looks east on Franklin Street from Second Street in 1895. The buildings on the left are part of the Hartenstein furniture and mortuary business. On the right is a hardware store that was operated by H. N. Kidd and Harry Hoffheins. Later Louis Zupnik operated a sewing factory in the building. Then Zacariah Alban ran a general store on the first floor and lived in the apartment on the second floor. The York County Sewing Factory was the last business operated here before the building was razed and the property turned into a parking lot for Crescent Industries.

This structure is one of the most recognized buildings in New Freedom. Arthur Hetrick built the structure in 1891. Maurice Spector bought the property in the early 1900s and operated a very popular department store. Levy Hirshman and Isaac Morris were the next owners. Then, Moul and Davis ran a variety store here. Later, an Acme grocery was on the first floor, and Norman (Dutch) Kiser had a variety store on the second floor.

When Acme left, Kiser moved his variety store to the first floor. Don and Joyce Moore had their dance studio in the building for a short time before Ed and Kay Hughes opened the Whistlestop Bike Shop in 1993. This picture of the old Spector's Department Store building was taken before the grade crossing at Franklin Street was installed. Behind the store is Israel Bailey's ice-cream factory and restaurant.

P. O. Klinefelter built this building 1891 on the northwest corner of East Second Street and West Main Street. The second floor was once used for band concerts and other town social functions. H. G. Bond, Frank Nonemaker, Wilmer King, and Arthur Zeller were the next owners. Charles "Todd" Kidd bought the store in the early 1930s. The next owner was Dick Hersey. Bob and Jean Hittie purchased the business in 1964 and operated it first as Pro Hardware and then as True Value Hardware. The building is now a violin and dance studio.

In this view looking north on North Second Street, Bob Hittie's pickup shows a Sherwin Williams emblem, which was New Freedom Hardware's paint line. The house behind the truck was later razed to provide a parking lot at the rear of New Freedom Hardware. The white building below the speed limit sign (10 North Second Street) was once Young and McNew's Barber Shop. Guns and sporting goods were also sold from this location.

The Farmers' Exchange was built by Milton W. Bahn in 1872. The presence of the wire cloth factory and the absence of the Mays Building indicate that this picture was taken between 1900 and 1909. Front Street is the dirt street between the main-line tracks and the spur on which the flatcar is sitting. The post office is through the double doors in the middle of the building. C. W. Zielger's Jewelry Store is through the door to the right.

This picture, taken after 1909, shows that the post office has moved from the double doors at left to the single door at right. The building was also used as a grain and feed business. Through the years, this building has been home to the Summit Service Station, Norris Richards' Dodge dealership, and currently, La Fontana Restaurant. The bunting on this building and on the department store to the right indicates that this picture was probably taken on a national holiday.

The McCauley Sewing Company started around 1895 along South Railroad Street. A second building was built about 1917, and the original structure was converted to a sorting room. The company made overalls that were worn by women working in the nearby fields. Employees are seen here modeling the overalls in 1917. The models are, from left to right, S. T. "Estie" Rohrbaugh (née Shue), unidentified, unidentified, Ada Koller, Grace Mays (née Miller), Jeanette Mundis (née Hoffacker), Agnes Shuchart (née Ryer), Edna Swartz, and Gladys Clarke (née Wilhelm). The buildings shown below still stand along South Railroad Street.

Daisy Montague and Robert Rohrbaugh bought the McCauley Sewing Company in 1934 and changed the name to the M&R Garment Company. These young ladies are M&R employees. They are standing on the south side of one of M&R's two buildings. M&R closed in 1972. It was the last of the New Freedom sewing factories. The house in the distance is the Arthur Zeller house at the corner Main and Railroad Streets.

A. N. Hetrick built a brick sewing factory on the east side of the New Freedom Wire Cloth factory at 21 East Franklin Street. W. H. Ziegler owned and operated the New Freedom Shirt Factory here for many years. The next owner of the factory was Louis Zupnick. It was sold to the American Insulator Company upon his death. The building was razed with the other American Insulator Company buildings. It stood on the lot on the west side of 23 East Franklin Street.

The advantage of a main-line railroad proved a boon to New Freedom industrial growth, including clothing manufacturing. The town's first sewing factory was on the second floor of Bailey's building at 1 East Main Street. Above, the employees of New Freedom Sewing Company gather for a picture in the summer of 1908. Below are some of the employees at their crowded work stations. There was enough work that some women sewed in their home. Each week, a wagon would bring the work to their home and pick up the work from the previous week.

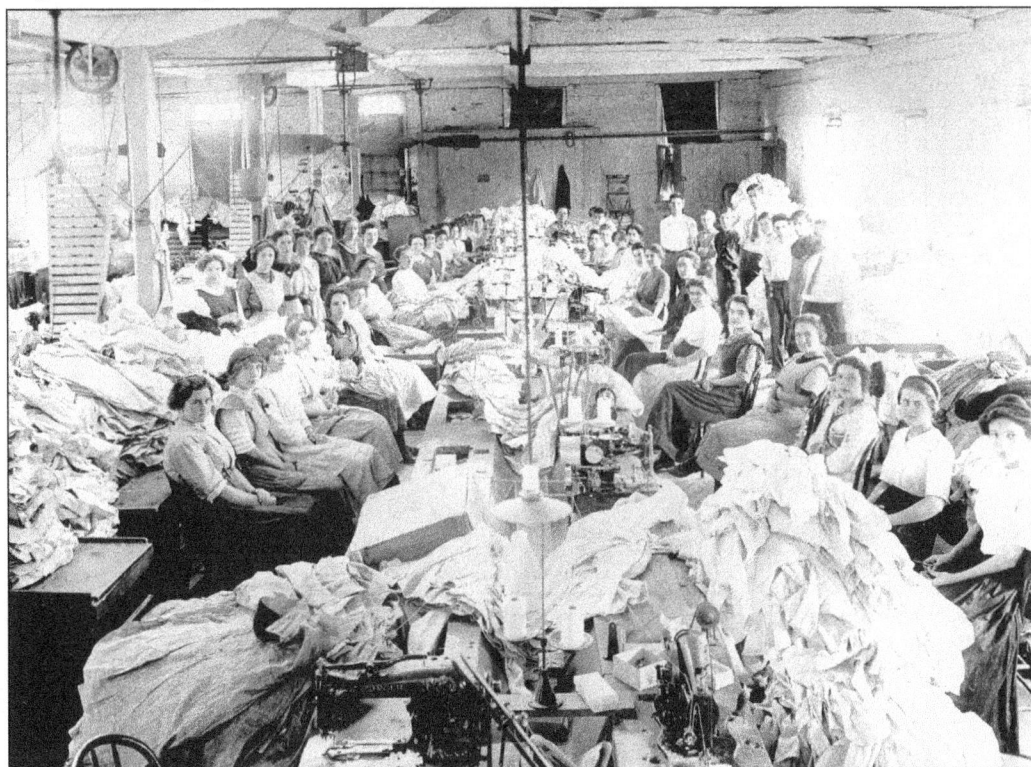

The first garage in New Freedom was started in 1913 by Howard Gemmill, a railroad supervisor. In 1920, Warner and Wirtz opened this garage in the Singer Building at 9 East Main Street. James Singer sold horses and buggies from this location, and Harvey Williams had a harness shop here. In later years, it was a machine shop, and part of it is now H&R Block.

In 1930, Warner and Wirtz moved into the red-brick garage and showroom on East Main Street. This picture was taken in 1948. Employees are, from left to right, as follows: (first row) Elvin Bailey, Harold Klinedinst, George Green, and Vernon Walker; (second row) George Wisner, Allen Wilson, Francis Klinedinst, Clair Starner, Melvin Rohrbaugh, Raymond Schminkey, Charles Warner, and Homer Starner. In later years, Richards Chevrolet and Oldsmobile operated from the same building.

Railroad engineer Jacob Mays built the Mays Building in 1909. Since that time, the building has seen dozens of businesses. G. H. Goodman bought the building in the late 1920s. The building has housed Itzoe's newsstand, Smith and Lambert Barber Shop, the Great Atlantic and Pacific Tea Company (A&P), Percy Allison's jewelry store, Hankin's Clothing Store, Dr. G. F. Stover's dentist office, White Hall Bank, La Motte's, and a bowling alley and pool hall.

This late-1920s photograph of the Mays Building shows the signs on two sides that identify it as now being owned by G. H. Goodman. The A&P is the largest business in the building. From left to right are Mrs. G. H. Goodman, Mrs. Amos Shetrone, John F. Lambert, Robert M. Smith, Amos Shetrone, Jake Taylor, Aaron Hankin, Frank Lutter, John Balkin, and Dr. G. F. Stover.

At one time, La Motte's was located on the second floor of the Mays Building. State regulations prohibiting the cohabitation of beer sales and recreation (pool hall) caused the restaurant to be moved downstairs to the banquet room. When A&P vacated the space, the restaurant moved into its present location on the first floor. La Motte's serves a variety of food, but it is best known for its delicious lump meat crab cakes.

The New Freedom Light and Power Company was chartered in 1901. It was located at 12 South Front Street, where the old firehouse stands today. Coal to operate the facility was carried across Front Street by wheelbarrow. The plant was sold to Glen Rock Light and Power in 1921, which later merged with Metropolitan Edison Company (MetEd). From left to right are John Bloss, George Hauff, Sylvester Walker, Ignatius Ebauer, unidentified, unidentified, Park Hedrick, George Schlaline, John Hoffman, Samuel Lloyd, Albert Wineholt, William Fourham, and Charles Ebaugh.

Another business that took advantage of the town's access to the rails was the New Freedom Wire Cloth Factory, which opened in 1900. It employed about 75 people in the manufacture of screening. In 1916, the wire cloth business was moved to Mount Wolf. Later in 1916, the American Insulator Company moved in and began operations.

The American Insulator Company used asbestos and pitch to custom mold small electrical and heat-resistance products. Some of the items produced at the factory were electrical insulating parts, radio knobs, radiator valve handles, gear shift knobs, radiator caps, knobs and handles for kitchen appliances and utensils, and, in later years, a variety of plastic products. The American Insulator Company closed its doors in 1986, and the buildings were razed a few years later.

Like the railroad, blacksmiths were very important to New Freedom's early development. They were the auto mechanics of their day. They provided the horseshoeing service to horse owners then, as tire salesmen provide service to car owners today. Above are Frank Hoak (left) and Lawrence Keller (right) about 1920. Below, as in yesteryear, blacksmiths exist today, and New Freedom still has one. Bob Wineholt still maintains a blacksmith business at 27 Church Alley.

Jeremiah Smith built the Colonial Hotel on North Front Street in 1883. The hotel offered comfortable accommodations for non-business travelers and traveling salesmen alike. New Freedom was known as "the place to stay" among salesmen because of the Colonial Hotel. Shown in this 1900 picture is the owner, Frank Zeller Sr. (right). Zeller also operated a livery stable for his visitors where he provided horse and buggies for rent.

After his death, Frank Zeller Sr.'s son Frank Jr. continued the business. He sold the hotel to Tex A. Redness in 1950. W. N. Richards and Edgar Mellinger bought the hotel in 1958. Today it is owned by Dennis Bazuine and called the Hodle Tavern.

Jeremiah Reehling established a butcher shop on East Franklin Street in the white structure now attached to the Mays Building (La Motte's). George T. Reehling later took over the business and moved it to 6 East Main Street. William H. Brenneman, and later his son Elmer, took over the business from Reehling and added seafood as a major part of the business. In later years, the building housed the New Freedom Laundromat, Frank's Pizza, and Mamma's Pizza. It is now Paesano Brothers' Pizza.

Elmer Brenneman used this truck to deliver groceries, produce, meat, and seafood around the area. From left to right are Ruth Russell, Ernest Russell, Elmer Brenneman, and Mary Billet (mother of Ruth Russell). This picture was taken in front of 214 North Constitution Avenue.

46

Like any small town, New Freedom had its share of small mom-and-pop businesses. Zackie Alban opened a small neighborhood grocery store in 1924 at the corner of West Main Street and Second Street. After the store closed, Lloyd Wagner TV and Appliances and then Bunny's TV Service operated from the building. New Freedom Hardware is on the far side of Alban's, and New Freedom Pharmacy is on the near side. Dr. Tom Penn ran New Freedom Pharmacy from 1960 to 1976. It has also been a video store and is now the home of Omni Graphics Microfilm Imaging.

A closer view of Alban's Grocery shows that it was originally a house that had a storefront added to it. Gladys Alban later assumed the business from Zackie and operated it until the 1960s, when the business closed.

Hilda Alban, sister of owner Gladys, stands behind the counter of Alban's in December 1962. On the shelves are a variety of different products sold in the store, such as toothpaste, stick licorice, Listerine, Pepto-Bismol, Tootsie Rolls, Palmolive shaving cream, aspirin, cigars, and chewing tobacco. A limited number of each item is on the shelves, unlike the large quantities found on the shelves of today's mega-stores.

At the rear of 17 West Main Street (Alban's Grocery), John Alban operated a coal delivery business. During the days of coal stoves and furnaces, people depended on reliable coal delivery to their homes to provide cooking and heating fuel. After the coal was burned, the ashes needed to be disposed of. Some residents dumped them in their garden for fertilizer. Others spread them in dirt alleys, and yet others depended on someone to haul them away.

Dr. H. A. Stover opened his first drugstore in 1909 in the newly built Mays Building. Later, he bought the house at 15 West Main Street, which had been built in 1868, and added a storefront to the house. Here, he opened another drugstore, which remained open for many years. Shown here is Dr. Stover holding his niece, Blanche Walters Martin, in front of the drugstore.

In this early-1900s photograph, Blanche Stover waits to be served on a stool at the soda fountain in Stover's Drug Store in the Mays Building. On the wall is a predominantly displayed Coca-Cola sign. Soda, or soda pop, was a novelty when it was first invented in Atlanta in May 1886. Today, there are dozens of different brands that we take for granted.

This soda fountain is at Stover's Drug Store at 15 West Main Street. It appears that Dr. Stover moved the marble-top fountain bar and stools from the Mays Building when he relocated. Again, Coca-Cola advertisements are behind the bar. This location was operated as a drugstore until 1976. In later years, it was New Freedom Pharmacy.

In 1874, Dr. Jeremiah Hedrick started his medical practice and drugstore at 100 East Main Street. The wooden structure on the left side of his brick home was added to provide office space and room for the store. This building still stands today on the southeast corner of East Main Street and South Constitution Avenue; it is now a private residence. The brick portion of the structure is alleged to have been moved to its present location from the top of the hill near where the community center is now.

In days of glass milk bottles and home milk delivery, Warner's Dairy truck was one of the familiar sights on New Freedom streets. Warner's Dairy was founded in 1903 in Red Lion. Warner's merged with Rutter's Dairy in the 1970s. Shown here is Lamar Carman in his 1973 New Freedom centennial get-up.

In this view looking west on East Franklin Street in the mid-1960s, D. A. Bostic's electrical appliance store is on the left. Two doors down is the New Theatre, now Bonkey's Ice Cream. *The Sound of Music*, released in 1965, is shown on the marquee. In the distance on the left is the New Freedom Department Store.

Lamar Carman ran a small store and ice-cream stand from the rear of his house on the northeast corner of East Main Street and North Constitution Avenue from 1950 to 1976. The store was in the white attachment to the rear of the house. This was a popular afternoon stopping place for kids coming down the hill from school. As part of their business, they also operated a milk delivery service in town. Pictured to the left is Ralph Carman (father of Lamar) beside their delivery truck. The milk delivery business operated from 1934 to 1992.

Looking west on East Franklin Street, D. A. Bostic's store is on the left. On the right just behind the fire trucks are two American Insulator Company buildings. In the distance beyond the Mays Building is the old Hartenstein furniture building and mortuary. This picture was taken from 38 East Franklin Street, where Vera McCullough originally operated her beauty salon.

This view looks north along the west side of the New Freedom Light and Power Company building. The Wesley Koller house (large white porch) is in the distance. The Koller house stood on the north side of West Main Street, and the New Freedom Light and Power building stood on the west side of South Front Street. Park Hedrick is the man standing beyond the wheelbarrow.

In 1904, the First National Bank of New Freedom was built on ground that the bank had purchased from Charles W. and Ann M. Koller. The purchase also led to the opening of Broad Street. The view below is from the front of Alban's Grocery. The empty field beyond the bank building is where Rutter's is today. Besides the First National Bank of New Freedom, the building has also housed the Commonwealth National Bank and Mellon Bank. Today it is home to Shaw Surveying.

This view looks east on Main Street from the Bubb Building. On the left is a Sunoco sign displayed by Summit Service. The white building on the left just across the tracks was the restaurant and residence of Clay Hughes, which burned down in 1958. To the lower right is an air force recruiting poster beside the entrance to the gift shop owned by Lucille Duerr. On the right side just across the track is the crossing watchman's shed, and behind that is Brenneman's.

This is the inside of Clay Hughes's establishment at 1 East Main Street. It is probably in the late 1940s or early 1950s, as evidenced by the small television on the wall behind the bar. Cigars, pipes, and pipe tobacco were also sold here. Clay Hughes's place was one of a couple in town where you could stop after work for a cold one and some conversation.

This is a late-1800s view of Miller's Mill, the site of Torbert's Store, located on East Main Street, east of Spector's Department Store and across the street from the baseball field that once occupied the ground that the American Insulator Company occupied. The mill stood on the ground now occupied by Fox's Pizza, in the same building where Nardie Young operated his grocery business for many years.

KOLLER & KUGLER,

—PROPRIETORS OF NEW FREEDOM—

LUMBER YARD.

Constantly on hand a large line of Building Lumber, consisting of

SIDING, FLOORING, DOORS, SASH,

CYPRESS AND PINE SHINGLES, WAINSCOTING,

FRAMING, DOOR AND WINDOW FRAMES,

PLASTERING LATHS. ALSO FENCING BOARDS AND PALINGS.

NEW FREEDOM, PA.

New Freedom's first lumber business was operated by Robert Koller. Later, the business became Koller and Kugler Lumber Company. O. C. Shirey and Joe Dice started the Summit Lumber Company in 1913. In 1936, Chester E. Rehmeyer took over the business and changed the name to New Freedom Lumber. Al George was the next operator, and then Allen Bull owned it. Dick Baade bought New Freedom Lumber in 1975 and moved it to Hungerford in 1988. The business closed in the late 1990s.

This pre–World War I steam-powered machine was owned by the Shuchart family of Maryland, and it was moved from farm to farm during the height of the harvest season. The machine was used to power a number of other devices used to thresh and to bale hay and straw, saw wood, grade roadways, and pull out hedge fences.

Another rail enthusiast uses the abandoned rails in New Freedom. To the right is Huckleberry's Restaurant, which was in business. Before Huckleberry's, the building was occupied by Mr. Bill's Seafood Restaurant. Mr. Bill's left New Freedom in the 1980s, moved to the Leader Heights exit on Interstate 83, and became Bill's Quarterdeck. After Huckleberry's, another restaurant had a short stay in the building. The building is now occupied by A Child's Place day care.

J. P. Hoffacker ran New Freedom's first cannery near the intersection of Singer Road and High Street. Louis P. Colgan built another cannery in 1916 on the lower portion of High Street. George Ruhl and Harry Freed bought the company but ran it for only a few years. Charles G. Summers Jr., his son Stran, and his son-in-law Frank Corse bought the company in 1923.

This 1929 photograph shows the cannery before it was destroyed by fire during the winter of 1932–1933. The plant was quickly rebuilt and back in operation in 1933. During World War II, German prisoners of war, who were interned in a camp in Stewartstown, were transported daily to work in the plant. After World War II, men came from Puerto Rico to work in the plant and in the fields. Mechanization of the plant in the mid-1960s reduced the need for the migrant workforce.

The Charles G. Summers Jr. Inc. cannery shipped numerous vegetable products under the Superfine label. Some of the many products were corn, peas, okra, lima beans, triple succotash, onions, tomatoes, and carrots. This vinery facility, shown here in 1949, would later become a health facility after the cannery merged with Hanover Foods and closed.

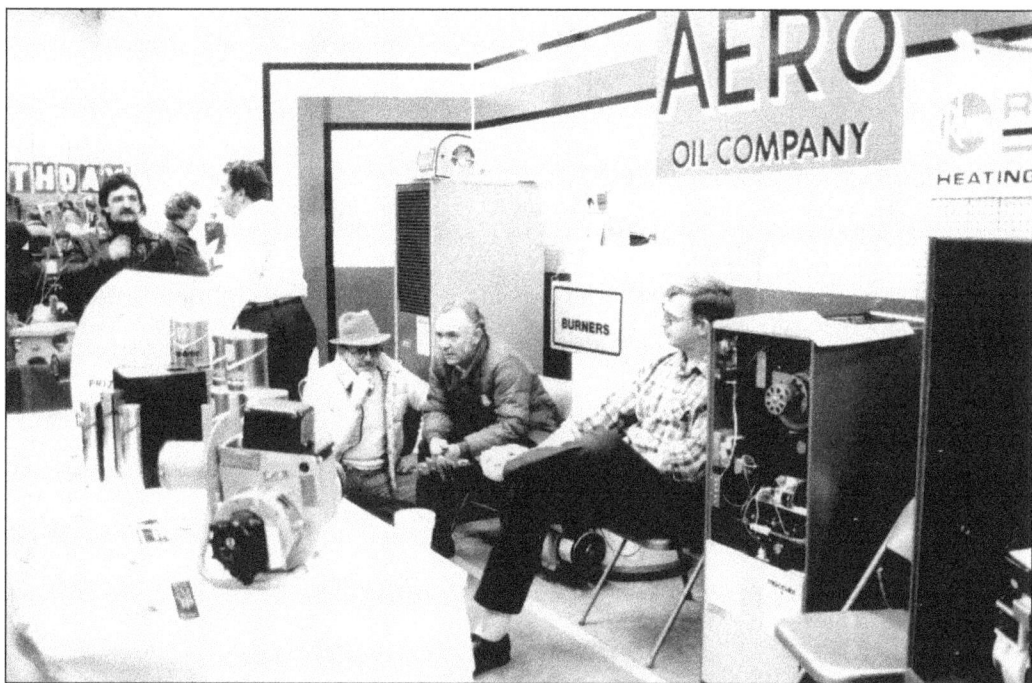

The New Freedom Business Show, an annual event held at the New Freedom Community Center and Fire Hall, provides local businesses the opportunity to promote themselves. Tables are set up by companies in real estate, banking, hardware, appliances, photography, crafts, automotives, home improvement, and various public services. The show is attended by residents of New Freedom and the surrounding communities.

These are tokens that were used by the Charles G. Summers Jr. Company and its predecessor, Ruhl and Freed Company, to pay their employees. The different shapes and sizes denoted different denominations. Local stores would accept the tokens from the workers in exchange for groceries or dry goods. The local merchants would then get reimbursed by turning the tokens in to the appropriate employer. This method of payment ensured that the money stayed in the local economy.

Four

UP AND DOWN
THE STREETS

Mr. and Mrs. Joseph Freeland stand in front of their residence at 101 West Penn Street. Joseph Freeland was instrumental in the organization of the New Freedom Equitable Building and Loan Association and the New Freedom Cemetery Association. He was also the director of the New Freedom Electric Light and Power Company, and for a time, he owned a bakery in town. The residence still stands today.

This three-story red-brick home was built at 103 West Penn Street. It was the home of Mr. and Mrs. Jesse Baughman. Mrs. Baughman was the daughter of Dr. and Mrs. Samuel Bailey, a veterinarian.

This is the house on 15 West Main Street that Dr. H. A. Stover bought and then moved his pharmacy to from the Mays Building. The doctor added a storefront and used the location as his new pharmacy. In later years the building would become New Freedom Pharmacy, a video store, and Omni Graphics Microfilm Imaging.

German immigrant Mathias Lutter built this house at 116 North Front Street in 1876 and operated a shoe business from there. In 1894, Mathias turned the business over to his son John, who operated it at another location on Front Street until he died in the 1950s. In later years, Helen Frantz, John's daughter and Mathias's granddaughter, lived in the house with her husband. The house is still a private residence but no longer in the Lutter family.

This house, at 29 East Main Street, is believed to be the oldest house in New Freedom. It was built in 1860 and was the home of Dr. Eli Free, who was the son of Peter Free and the grandson of Conrad Free. Dr. Free practiced medicine in New Freedom from 1860 to 1890. Eli's three brothers—Adam, Jared, and John—were also physicians.

This was Wesley Koller's house on West Main Street in 1915. The house stood on the north side of West Main Street, across from the New Freedom Light and Power Company building and between the Farmers' Exchange and Dr. Yagle's house. Wesley Koller supplied the horses to the Rose Fire Company for its horse-drawn fire wagon.

This was Dr. James Yagle's house on West Main Street. The house was built by Milton Bahn in 1890. Dr. Yagle practiced medicine in New Freedom from 1902 until he died in the 1950s. This building still stands, and it is one of the best-known structures on West Main Street.

This is the Bowser farmhouse. The bell on the pole is in front of what was known as the Bowser Bake Ovens. From left to right are an unidentified hired girl, Mrs. Samuel (Saville) Bowser, Mrs. Benjamin (Laura) Bowser, Benjamin Bowser, Howard Bowser, and Harry King. The Bowser farm was located on the west side of town and was known as Bloomfield.

This is Amos Baughman's farmhouse. Baughman was a drover who dealt in horses and mules that he imported from the West and sold locally. He was a prominent businessman in town and active in town politics. His grandson Clarence was once chief burgess of New Freedom. Standing on the porch are, from left to right, Maria Baughman (Mrs. William Day), Margaret Baughman (Mrs. John Donaldson), and Mrs. Amos Baughman.

This wood-frame residence, built before 1840, was the home of Meinrad Muller. The first Catholic mass was said in this house in 1841. Muller later donated the land on the east side of Shrewsbury Road (Constitution Road) where the first Catholic church was built. The King family later acquired this house, which still stands at the intersection of North Constitution Avenue and Pleasant Avenue. In the photograph are the King family members. From left to right are Lillie McDonald (née King), Mabel Downs (née King), Wayne King, Ada King, T. Arthur King, and Wilmer King.

This early-1900s view shows some of the first houses built on Third Street. The first house (left) was built by Chester Kugler. The second house was built by a Mr. and Mrs. Shaffer, who were son-in-law and daughter of John Grove, who built the third house. The fourth house was built by Ross McCubbins. These houses were built around 1900 and, although extensively remodeled over the years, still stand today.

FRANKLIN ST. NEW FREEDOM

The view above looks east on East Franklin Street in 1911. The street and sidewalk are still dirt. These recently built homes were just east of the New Freedom Wire Cloth Factory. The pipes at the left indicate that either a water system or sewage system was being installed. The view below is from 1916. The street and sidewalks have been paved, and trees and shrubs have been planted around the houses. Curiously, most of the utility poles are missing, probably removed from the photograph for aesthetics. Someone standing on this spot today would see several of the utility poles leaning in a similar fashion as to those in the above photograph.

This early-1900s postcard view looks east on East Main Street. Concrete sidewalks have been installed, but the street have not yet been paved. Beyond the intersection with Shrewsbury Road (now North Constitution Avenue), the street narrows to a wide path, and there are no sidewalks. Children had to walk on East Main Street up and down the hill as they went to and from school.

This view from the late 1800s is looking west on Main Street from the area of the old school (now the community center). The porch roof on Dr. Jeremiah Hedrick's home can be seen on the left. The roof to the right among the trees is on the Ward house, which was built on the northeast corner of East Main Street and Shrewsbury Road.

We are looking north on Shrewsbury Road before the road was paved and the newer houses were built on the left. The road was renamed Constitution Avenue about 1944. The name was chosen to give it a patriotic flavor. Up until the 1960s, the road ended at a T intersection with the Susquehanna Trail. When the Southern Farms development and Market Square were built, Old Farm Lane was built to provide access.

Looking west on Main Street in 1900 from Center Square, this view shows the house built by Milton W. Bahn on the right. The house later served as the residence and office of Dr. J. L. Yagle. On the near left is the bakery of Bunkle and Lau, later Peoples Baking Company. The house was later remodeled by adding a storefront. Bee's Hive Restaurant was on the first floor of the house, and apartments were on the second floor. Beyond the house is the steeple on St. John's Lutheran Church. The pickle tree standing in the yard is a fairly rare variety, and there are only a few of this type tree in the area.

The Junior Order of United American Mechanics (JOUAM) building was built at 123 West Main Street on land donated by Milton W. Bahn in 1895. Several other organizations used the hall, including the Daughters of America and the New Freedom Equitable Building and Loan Association. In 1918, the Sylvania Theater opened on the second floor. It operated until the New Theater opened on East Franklin Street in 1941.

The New Freedom Veterans of Foreign Wars (VFW Post 7012) was formed in 1946. The post bought the JOUAM hall in 1948. The second floor was removed and a brick façade added during extensive renovation of the building. VFW Post 7012 still operates today in the hall that barely resembles the original structure.

The New Freedom Library was organized by the Women's Club in 1968 at 8 South Front Street. In 1973, the library moved to larger facilities at 4–6 South Front Street. It remained at that location until October 2003, when it merged with the Shrewsbury Public Library to form the Southern York County Library at 80 Constitution Avenue in Shrewsbury.

Jail, New Freedom, Pa.

Looking south along the main line of the railroad, this view shows the town jail, which sat between the tracks and South Front Street behind J. D. Bailey's building (now the feed mill). The jail had a small window with iron bars and a solid door. It was used to lock up vagrants who would drift into town aboard trains.

When he owned the Colonial Hotel, Frank Zeller Sr. also operated a nearby livery stable. The livery business was convenient for the traveling salesmen who rode into town on the rails and stayed at the hotel. The salesmen would rent horses and buggies while they peddled their wares around town. In the picture are, from left to right, S. A. Zeller, John F. Lambert, John Zeller, and Spencer Housman.

On the west side of the railroad, across the Singer Road Bridge, was the John Ryer farm, shown in this 1910 picture. John's son Francis Ryer was the next owner of the farm, and later Francis's son John owned the farm. The farm still exists. On the east side of the railroad tracks was the Bailey farm, which is now a housing development.

The cabinetmaking and undertaking business was conducted by David Hershey in a shop at 40 East Main Street. After Hershey died in 1885, the business was taken over by George L. Hartenstein, who moved the business to 100 North Front Street. Paul N. Hartenstein and Curvin H. Nonemaker bought the business in 1905 and called it Old Reliable Furniture and Carpet House. In 1910, the name was changed to Hartenstein and Company.

This 1930s view shows the Hartenstein building after it had been remodeled and a mortuary chapel added on the right. After the furniture business closed, the undertaking business was moved into a new building on the corner of Franklin and Second Streets. After years of standing vacant, the old building was razed in the 1970s. The woodshop behind the main building was razed in the 1980s. The lot is now owned by Trinity United Methodist Church.

Rose Fire Company No. 1 was chartered in New Freedom on May 1, 1905. Why the name Rose was chosen is still debated. The photograph above shows the dedication of the fire company in 1912. The fire company's first equipment was limited to hand-carried hoses, a few buckets, and some wrenches. Later, fire equipment was transported by wagon. The picture below shows the christening of the town's new fire wagon. The small girl is Catherine (Rohrbaugh) Fisher, the wagon driver is Wesley Koller, and the man standing is Rev. John Bowers. Koller donated the use of the horses that pulled the fire wagon.

Charter members of the New Freedom Fire Company are shown here. The horse rider at left is unidentified. The others are, from left to right, as follows: (first row) Charles Koller Sr., Melvin Day, Robert Bollinger, John Koller, Dr. George S. Stone, William Lowe, unidentified, unidentified, Charles Cooper, John Zeller Sr., Aaron Reehling, unidentified, J. D. Miller, William Miller (past postmaster), and John Lutter Sr.; (second row) Peter Shuchart, unidentified, A. B. Kugler, unidentified, Thomas McCullough, P. O. Klinefelter, Frank Ziegler, William Ziegler, unidentified, Jesse (Jumbo) Miller Sr. (flag bearer), John Hoffacker, Oscar Hunter, unidentified, Harold Gemmill, Wilbur King, Roland Baughman, Thomas Gale, M. S. Painter, unidentified, Jacob Mays, and H. G. Bond (in buggy).

Fire companies take pride in the quality and the appearance of their fire vehicles. Parades have long been the occasion for fire companies to show off the equipment and fire personnel. This early-1900s photograph is an example of how long Rose Company No. 1 has participated in local parades.

The New Freedom Fire Company has always been a volunteer organization. Its ladies' auxiliary was formed in 1939. The company has long depended upon fund-raising and donations to keep it well equipped. In 1937, the Charles G. Summers Jr. Inc. cannery donated a booster tank to better enable the company to fight commercial building fires. In 1934, the ambulance at right was donated to the fire company.

As New Freedom grew, so did Rose Fire Company. By the 1950s, the company had three trucks, a utility vehicle, and an ambulance. The company now has mutual-aid agreements with fire companies throughout much of York County and Carroll and Harford Counties, Maryland.

Rose Fire Company has long provided the primary ambulance service for New Freedom, Shrewsbury, Railroad, and much of the surrounding southern York County area. Now, with modern equipment, the Rose Fire Company ambulance responds to about 1,200 ambulance calls annually.

ROSE FIRE CO. No. 1

The first fire station was located in a two-story building on Second Street. In 1922, the fire company moved to the vacant building of the former New Freedom Light and Power Company. In 1937, the firehouse was replaced by this two-story brick building at the same location at 12 South Main Street. As the town grew, so did the fire company. By 1975, it was necessary to move the firehouse to its present location on East Main Street.

Youth for Christ was a Christian program for young people in the New Freedom area. It was active from 1950 to 1971 and met in the community center, which at that time was on the second floor of the New Freedom Fire Station at 12 South Main Street. Lamar and Ruth Carman sponsored the program.

Postal service in New Freedom was established on January 31, 1851. Over the years, the post office was located in various building in town, mostly around Center Square, including the Farmers' Exchange and at 4 East Main Street. The post office moved to its present location at 5 South Broad Street in October 1959.

Pictured here is a special cover issued by the New Freedom post office in 1973 to commemorate the town's bicentennial. The envelope shows the official bicentennial seal and caricatures of the train station and the old town jail. This particular cover was canceled on May 1, 1973, the 68th anniversary of Rose Fire Company.

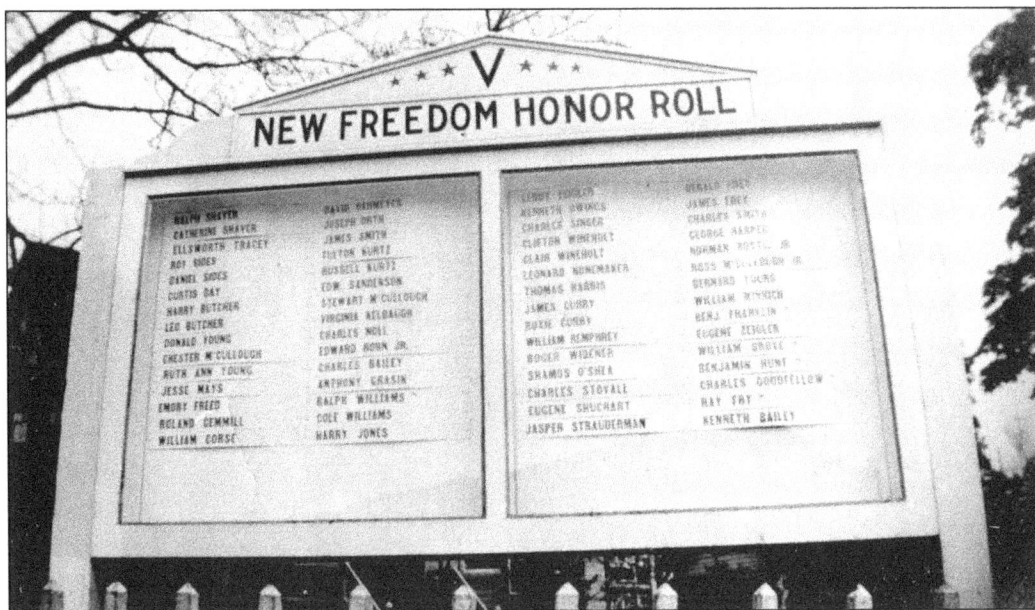

NEW FREEDOM HONOR ROLL

RALPH SHAVER	DAVID DEHMEYER	LEROY FULOLER	GERALD PACK
CATHERINE SHAVER	JOSEPH ORTH	KENNETH BROOKS	JAMES TREX
ELLSWORTH TRACEY	JAMES SMITH	CHARLES SINGER	CHARLES SMITH
ROY RODES	CLIFTON KURTZ	CLIFTON WINEHOLT	GEORGE HARPER
DANIEL SIPES	RUSSELL KURTZ	CLAIR WINEHOLT	NORMAN ROYER JR.
CURTIS DAY	EDW. SANDERSON	LEONARD NONEMAKER	ROSS M'CULLOUGH JR.
HARRY BUTCHER	STEWART M'CULLOUGH	THOMAS HARRIS	BERNARD YOUNG
LEE BUTCHER	VIRGINIA RELDAUGH	JAMES CURRY	WILLIAM RINEICH
DONALD YOUNG	CHARLES NOLL	RUTH CURRY	BENJ. FRANKLIN
CHESTER M'CULLOUGH	EDWARD HORN JR.	WILLIAM REMPHREY	EUGENE ZEIGLER
RUTH ANN YOUNG	CHARLES BAILEY	ROGER WIDENER	WILLIAM GROVE
JESSE MAYS	ANTHONY GRASIN	SHAMOS O'SHEA	BENJAMIN HUNT
EMORY FREED	RALPH WILLIAMS	CHARLES STOVALL	CHARLES GOODFELLOW
ROLAND GEMMILL	COLE WILLIAMS	EUGENE SHUCHART	RAY FRY
WILLIAM CORSE	HARRY JONES	JASPER STRAUDERMAN	KENNETH BAILEY

The New Freedom Honor Roll, located in the town square, listed the names of 60 New Freedom residents who served in the American armed forces during World War II. Below are four soldiers from New Freedom who got together in Boston on November 20, 1944, before they shipped overseas. The soldiers are, from left to right, Red Landis, Charles Seitz, Jesse Mays, and Stewart C. "Doc" Bowers.

Upon return from military service at the end of World War II, many former servicemen formed or joined fraternal veteran organizations like the American Legion, the Veterans of Foreign Wars, and the American Veterans. Marching units from these organizations were a common sight in holiday parades on Memorial Day, the Fourth of July, Labor Day, and Veterans Day. This parade of veterans is shown marching west on East Main Street near the school (now the community center).

Holiday parades were usually led by military honor guards. These men are members of the New Freedom Veterans of Foreign Wars first honor guard. From left to right are Dean Baughman, Medford Smith, Jack Frederick, and Charles Goodfellow.

Like many towns in Pennsylvania, New Freedom supplied its share of men to serve in World War I. This get-together of local veterans was held at the home of Bill Smith (standing second from right) about a mile west of town. Harold Moody (standing at left) was a correspondent for the York Gazette and Daily. Dr. S. Cole Bowers (civilian clothes) continued his medical practice in town until he died in 1969. Charles M. (Todd) Kidd (on crutches), who was severely wounded, worked for New Freedom Light and Power Company for a time and then operated New Freedom Hardware until he retired. Arthur Zeller Sr. (next to Todd) worked in a die shop at American Insulator Company until he retired.

Boy Scouts from Troop 24, New Freedom, served as attendants to Civil War veterans at the 75th and last reunion of the Blue and Gray at Gettysburg during the week of July 4, 1938. Among the New Freedom Scouts were Robert Franklin, Benjamin Franklin, George La Motte, Shamos O'Shea, Edward Sanderson, and Roland Gemmill. Shown here are, from left to right, Roland Gemmill, Newton Harmon, and Edward Sanderson. Harmon, from Lewistown, enlisted in the Union army at age 16 and fought at Gettysburg. The neckerchiefs worn by the Scouts were blue and gray.

There were nearly 2,000 veterans at the 75th anniversary reunion. Their average age was in the 90s, and most of them needed assistance getting from place to place. The Scouts spent over a week at Gettysburg caring for the needs of the aged veterans. Shown here carrying water are Jesse Mays (left) and Robert Franklin.

The New Freedom Farmer's Fair, forerunner of the New Freedom Carnival, was held annually in September from 1900 until about 1918. Large canvas tents were erected in the woods close to the public school, now known as the Mervin Smith Woods. Farmers and businessmen used the tents to display agricultural and commercial goods. Games and amusements were also provided for the children. This picture was taken about 1914.

Forest Lakes is a secluded lakeside residential area about two miles east of New Freedom in southern York County. Often thought of as part of Shrewsbury, the homes at Forest Lakes are on the New Freedom rural mail delivery route. Forest Lakes began in 1962 with the clearing of trees and the flooding of the farmland in the valley south of Windy Hill Road and east of

the Susquehanna Trail. The original concept for the area was to provide a weekend retreat of lakeside cottages for Baltimore area residents. The area soon became so popular that family homes were built to support year-round living. A second lake was added in 1973.

Above is an early-1960s view of the Forest Lakes area before the ground was flooded. The lower road running from left to right is now Magnolia Circle. The upper road running diagonally is Windy Hill Road. The farm buildings along Windy Hill Road were razed to provide for additional development on the east side of the lake. Below is a 1970s postcard view of the original lake. The lakes are used by the residents of Forest Lakes for swimming, boating, fishing, and ice-skating.

Five

RECREATION AND LEISURE

By the 1990s, it was obvious that the rail line from York to Baltimore was not going to be used again. Federal funds were available to convert abandoned rail lines into recreational trails. One such project was the NCR/York County Heritage Trail in Maryland and Pennsylvania. The trail is 41 miles long: 20 miles from Ashland Road in Baltimore County, Maryland, to the Mason-Dixon Line and 21 miles from the Mason-Dixon Line to the city of York. This picture shows the building of the trail through New Freedom.

Parades have always been a big event in small-town America. New Freedom is no exception. These pictures from New Freedom's centennial parade show how the town recognized the importance of the railroad in the town's history. The float to the left consists of a steam engine not unlike those that served as pusher engines to help trains over the summit. The float below depicts the watchman's shed on Main Street.

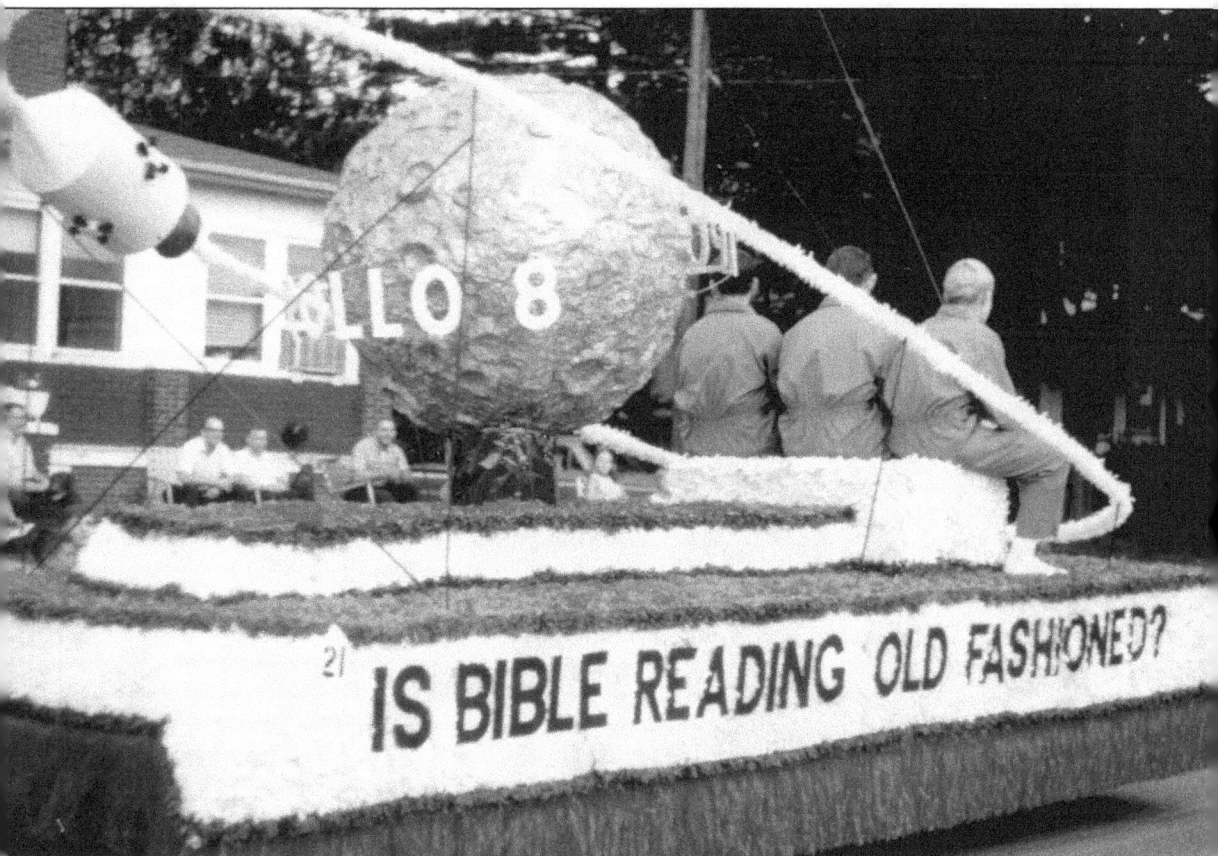

This New Freedom float, probably from a 1969 parade, pays homage to the Apollo 8 flight, which in December 1968 became the first manned flight to orbit the moon. During that flight, astronauts Frank Borman, Jim Lovell, and Bill Anders read passages from the Bible after they entered lunar orbit on Christmas Eve.

New Freedom celebrated its centennial during the week of August 11, 1973. The town celebrated opening day on August 11, Religious Heritage Day on August 12, Agricultural Day on August 13, Gemutlichkeit Day on August 14, Youth Day on August 15, Merchants and Industry Day on August 16, Homecoming Day on August 17, and Celebration Day on August 18. The queen of the centennial was Gail Lentz, shown here during the centennial parade.

During the days before radio, television, computers, and video games, townspeople found ways to make their own forms of entertainment. One such way was a local band. This view of the New Freedom Band was taken at the home of George F. and Leah Koller Miller. Band members are, from left to right, as follows: (first row) Howard Bailey, Walter Swartz, John Bailey, Stewart Rohrbaugh, Paul Strasbaugh, and John Harman; (second row) W. H. Freed, Howard Peterman, Benjamin Strasbaugh, Clarence Rohrbaugh, John Wildamuth, and James F. Singer; (third row) Ira S. Painter, John Schuppert, Harry Rohrbaugh, James I. Decker, J. D. Bailey, John Zeller, Ross McCubbin, and William H. Lowe.

Although not a scene from New Freedom, this view from Little Round Top in Gettysburg features a family from New Freedom. The vehicle is 1911 Pullman K-10 touring car built in York, Pennsylvania. The family members include George Howard Gemmill (owner and driver), Betty Schwartz (née Gemmill) (in front), Harry L. Gemmill Sr. (left rear), and Florence Gemmill (née Backman) (center rear).

Baseball was an important part of New Freedom's past. A team from New Freedom played in the Adams-York County Semi-Professional League for many years. Members of the 1900 team are, from left to right, as follows: (first row) Oscar Hunter, Ralph Day, unidentified, unidentified, and Ed Eckenrode; (second row) manager Oscar Bailey, Howard Gemmill, Howard Bollinger, Mont Koller, Stewart C. Bowers, Howard Miller, and Charles Lowe.

Pictured here is the New Freedom team of 1908. Team members are, from left to right, as follows: (first row) Russ McDonald, John Bailey, Frank Bowers, Harry La Motte, Jesse Miller, Irwin La Motte, and Ernie Ziegler; (second row) Jake Mays, scorer Jim Decker, Walter Bloss, Dick Strasbaugh, Guy Reehling, umpire Irwin Hamilton, and manager Oscar Bailey. The Zupnick Sewing Factory is the brick building in the background.

The 1912 New Freedom team of the Southern York County League is shown here. Team members are, from left to right, as follows: (first row) manager Oscar Bailey, John Bailey, Harry La Motte, Paul Strausbaugh, Erwin La Motte, Jesse Miller, and Stewart Rohrbaugh; (second row) Jake Mays, umpire Quiggle, Ernie Ziegler, Walter Bloss, Richard Strausbaugh, Frank Bowers, James Decker, John Bloss, and Oscar Hunter.

The New Freedom baseball team of 1917 poses for this photograph. Team members are, from left to right, as follows: (first row) unidentified, Willie La Motte, Ernie Ziegler, unidentified, and Stewart Rohrbaugh; (second row) Jesse Miller, ? Smith, Melvin Day, Guy Reehling, James Clancy, and ? Ketterman.

The New Freedom Ball Field was located on the north side of East Franklin Street between the Mays Building and the Zupnick Sewing Factory. The building in the background at left was the Torbert General Store. The building at right was the Dr. Hartenstein Building. The alley between the two buildings connects East Franklin Street and East Main Street. Dr. Hartenstein's

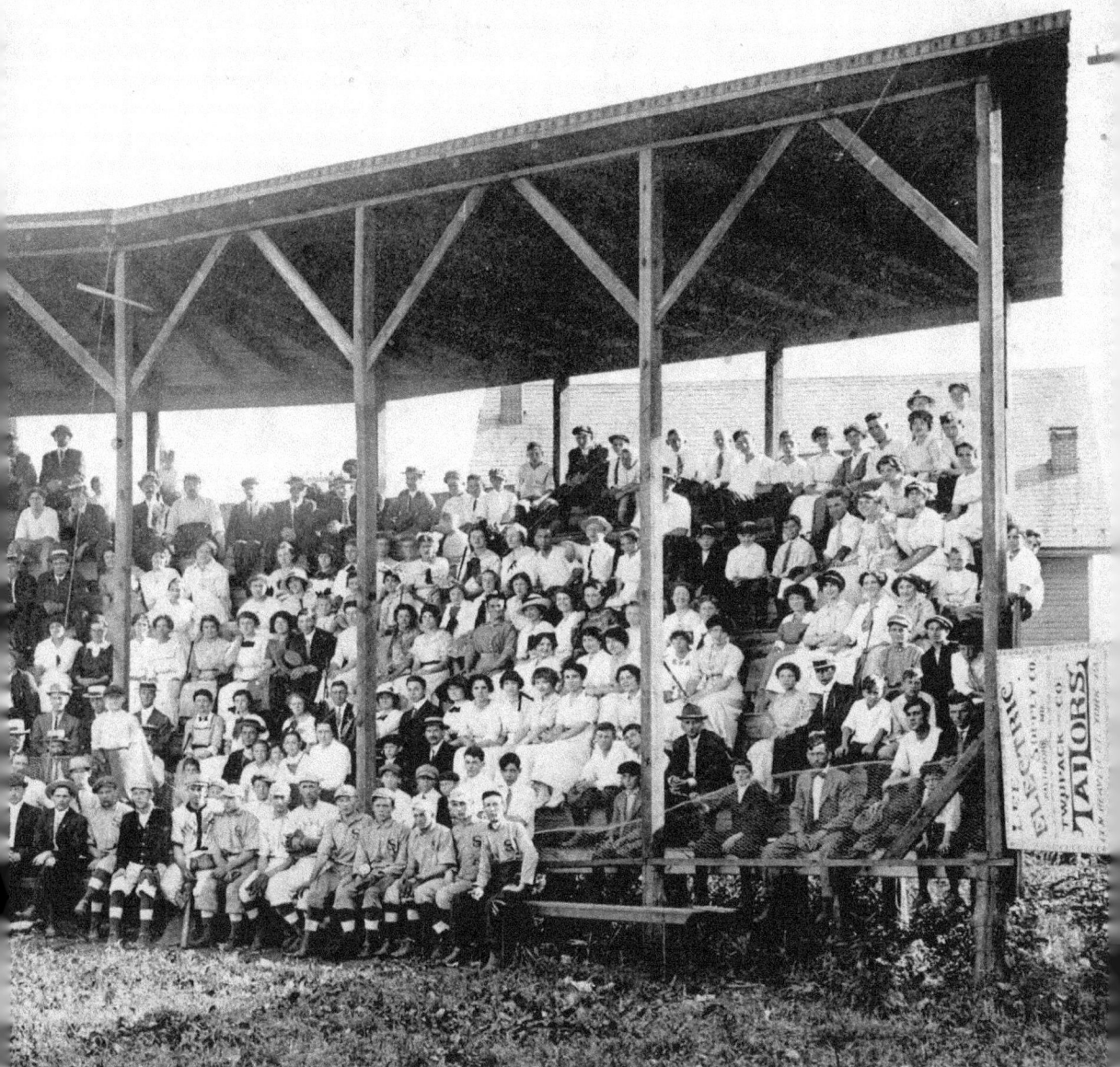

building was later razed to build Nardie's grocery store. The building is now Fox Pizza. When Jake Mays built the Mays Building, he included showers, lockers, and a clubhouse for the New Freedom team in the basement of the building.

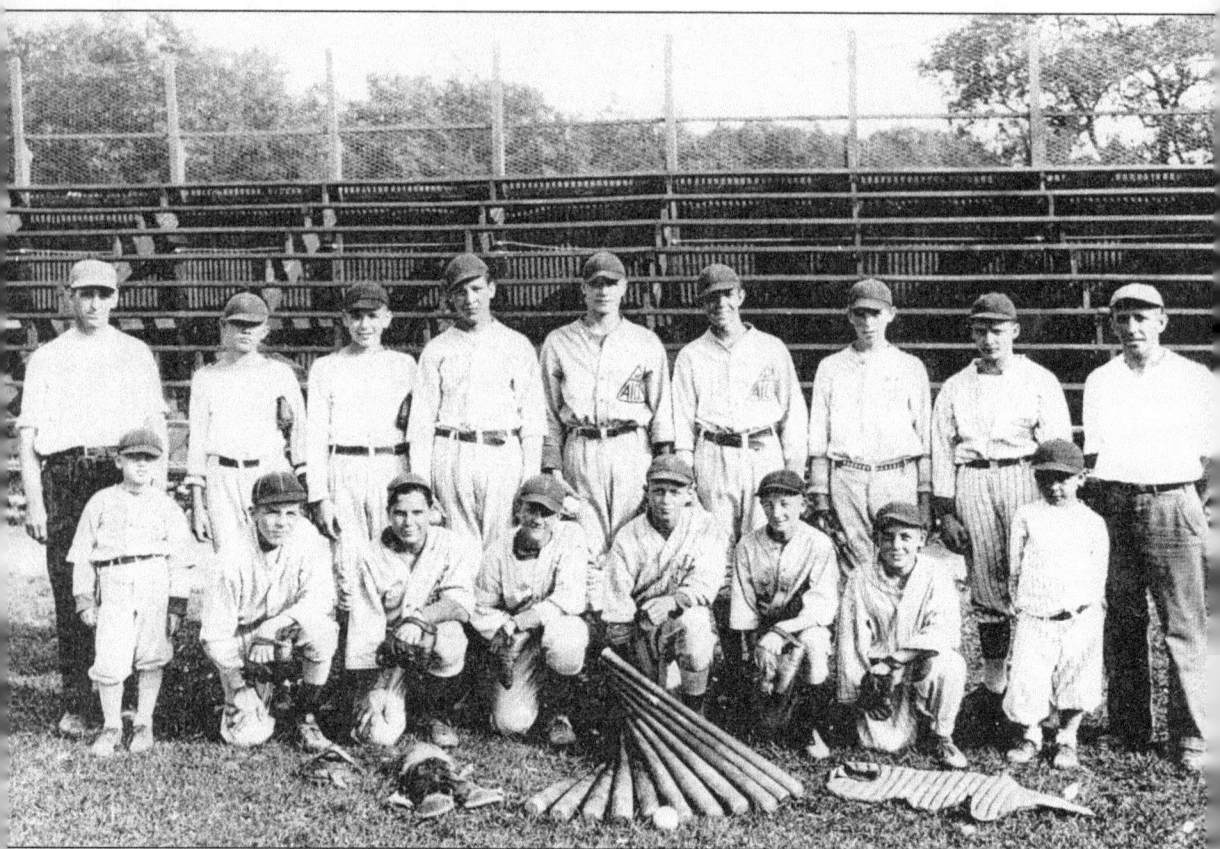

New Freedom's American Legion baseball champs of 1931 pose here. Team members, from left to right, are as follows: (first row) bat boy Dean Hamilton, Richard Strasbaugh, Frank Zellers, Stewart Butcher, Danny Bupp, Paul Brown, Donald Young, and bat boy Tyrus Young; (second row) manager Erwin La Motte, Fritz Hauff, James Smith, Jake Hartenstein, Stewart Bowers Jr., Harry Reehling, Maurice Zeigler, Lewis Hartenstein, and Mack Young.

The American Insulator Company also fielded a semiprofessional team in the Adams-York County Baseball League. The players were employees at the plant. The team's pitching staff from 1936 through 1941 are, from left to right, Joe Bierly Sr., Armand "Chick" Gladfelter, Curtis Day, and Jake Herman.

Other players for the American Insulator Company team in the Adams-York County Semi-Professional Baseball League are, from left to right, left fielder Barto Sweitzer Sr., right fielder Pete Wecker, and center fielder Bart Brown. These players played from 1936 through 1941. The American Insulator Company team played in the Pennsylvania Semi-Pro Baseball Tournament in 1939, 1940, and 1941 at Vandergrift, Pennsylvania.

This picture of Howard "Bubb" Miller (left) and Jesse Miller was taken about 1907 at their West Franklin Street home. Howard played on New Freedom's first team, which was organized at the beginning of the 20th century. Another brother, Walter, also played organized ball for New Freedom. At least one of the Miller brothers played every year during a 30-year period from 1899 to 1929.

New Freedom native Daniel Jesse Mays is one of 25 to 30 New Freedom area men who played professional baseball. Four of them received major-league baseball contracts. Jesse played minor-league ball in New Iberia, Louisiana, and Greenville, North Carolina, for an affiliate of the Pittsburgh Pirates. Mays is a member of the New Freedom High School Hall of Fame, World War II Bronze Star recipient, and the author of the book *100th Anniversary of Sports in Glen Rock, PA., 1894–1994*.

Above are New Freedom catchers Nelson "Nels" Mays (left), Harry "Hap" Trout (center), and William "Pug" Donahue. Donahue was an outstanding catcher for the American Insulator team for many years. He also managed New Freedom teams in the York County League and the York-Adams League. Many said that he likely would have been a major-league player if it had not been for his five-foot two-inch stature. He died on December 31, 1981. Below are fellow ballplayers who were his pallbearers. From left to right are Harry "Hap" Trout, Stewart "Doc" Bowers (Boston Red Sox), Kenny Raffensberger (four National League teams), Armond "Chick" Gladfelter, Joseph Hierley, Raymond Schuman, Harry "Hank" Sweeney, and Jess Mays.

In his early years, Bill Donahue Sr. became interested in magic after seeing performances by the great magician Harry Blackstone Sr. Bill developed a magic act and performed it many times to audiences in New Freedom and the surrounding area. He also operated a magic shop on the corner of Third and Franklin. Below, Bill is seen at his magic stand at the York County Fair.

Bill Donahue Sr. was a notary public and also served several six-year terms as justice of the peace in New Freedom. He started a printing business in 1950, which he relocated from Maryland Line to New Freedom in 1952. Bill Donahue III took over the printing business from his father in 1990 and continues to operate both the printing business and the magic shop on Third Street.

The New Freedom Carnival has long been an annual attraction that has brought the community together. The scene above shows the grounds where the carnival is held annually. The buildings closest to the trees are the former M&R Garment Company. An excursion passenger train can be seen moving north along the rail line. In the photograph below, the carnival is in full swing. The Lions Club–sponsored event is held annually in July. The finale is a huge fireworks display.

Six

THINGS ABOUT TOWN

Looking east from the top of the hill near Franklin and Third, this early-1900s view shows the New Freedom Wire Cloth Factory. The sanctuary has been added to the Methodist church, so it is after 1905. The Mays Building has not yet been built, so it is before 1909. The homes beyond W. H. Ziegler's New Freedom Shirt Factory (later owned by Louis Zupnick) have not been built on East Franklin Street. The top of Spector's Department Store can be seen on the south side of East Franklin Street. Hartenstein's Furniture Store can be seen behind the Methodist church. The vacant lot diagonally across Second Street from the church is now occupied by Hartenstein's Funeral Home.

This picture was taken about the same year as the one on the preceding page, but in a different season. With no leaves on the trees, more detail can be seen of the homes and businesses. East Franklin Street has not yet been paved, and the sidewalks are dirt paths. The New Freedom Public School can be seen in the distance on the hill on the east side of town.

The picture is of the same area as the previous two; however, numerous differences can be seen. The Mays Building has been completed, which dates this picture after 1909. Several houses have been built on the north side of East Franklin Street, east of the shirt factory. Improved sidewalks have been built along East Franklin Street, and the street has been paved. The building with the log roof, running right to left near the right edge of the picture, is on West Main Street and was once New Freedom Hardware Store.

This 1996 aerial view of the center of New Freedom shows the vacant lot that once was home to New Freedom Wire Cloth Factory, the town baseball field, and later, the American Insulator Company. It was also the location of a pond where ice was cut to be used for refrigeration in the icehouse at Bailey's ice-cream factory on North Railroad Street. The once busy railroad tracks are now used to store old passenger cars and cabooses. The train station can be seen in its deteriorated condition before it was dismantled and rebuilt. The vacant lot that is to the left of the farthest passenger cars, partially obstructed by the tree, is where Israel Bailey's and later Clay Hughes's restaurants stood.

This rare Spector's purse was purchased by a local resident on eBay, as was the Spector's dish to the right. These items are typical of the collectibles that were once produced by local merchants. The inside of the purse's lid contains an advertisement for Spector's Department Store in Glen Rock and in New Freedom. The advertisement mentions men's clothing tailored in Baltimore. The dish is rose colored, and the center states, "Compliments of Spector's Department Store."

A variety of novelty items were produced to commemorate New Freedom's centennial. Among the many items were cups, saucers, glasses, milk pitchers, dishes, ashtrays, mugs, bells, saltshakers, peppershakers, vases, piggy banks, tea sets, plaques, wooden nickels, and so forth. Most of the items are ceramic, but a few are pewter. Many of the items are one-of-a-kind because they were made as sample sales items in anticipation of mass production. Almost all of these items contained the official centennial seal. Many of the rare single items were rescued from a potential trash bin and are now safe in a local private collection.

Local businesses also offered commemoratives in recognition of New Freedom's centennial. The bakelite coaster to the right was produced at the American Insulator Company plant on East Franklin Street. The Superfine dish and the can bank were offered by Charles G. Summers Jr. Inc. on East High Street. Both are considered to be rare collectibles from New Freedom's past.

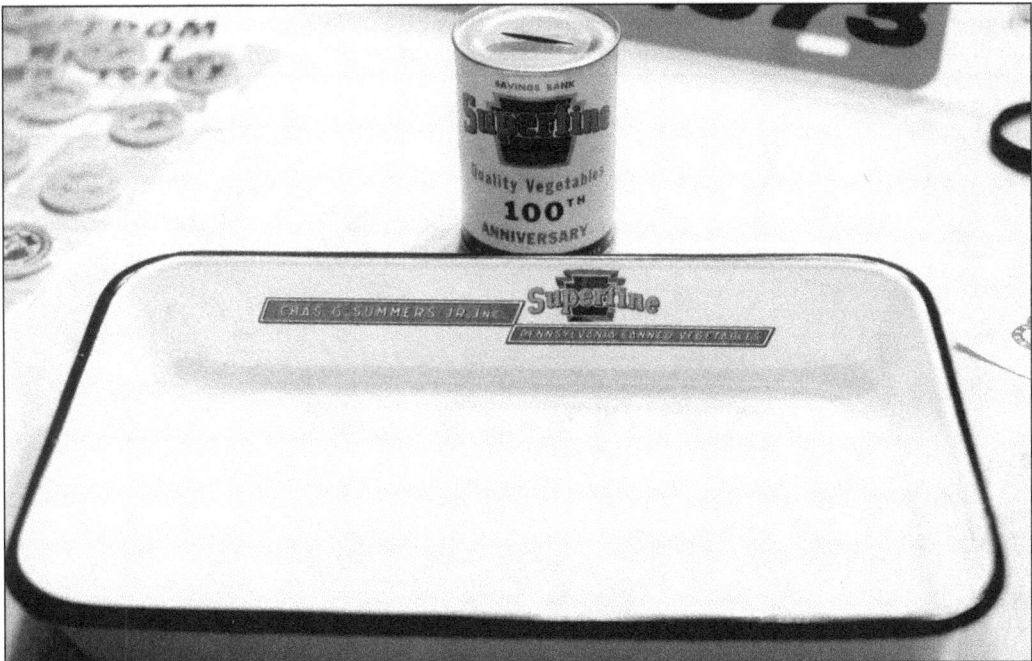

Above are three small games that were given to children as mementos of New Freedom's centennial. It is hard to believe that just 30 years ago, before video games and computers, children were still amused by such simple activities. Below is a collection of wooden nickels. Local merchants distributed the coins with their business logo or advertisement to their customers.

It is customary for the citizens of a town that commemorates a centennial, sesquicentennial, or bicentennial to dress in period clothing and participate in community activities as part of the celebration. New Freedom was no exception, as can be seen in this picture of Bob and Jean Hittie as they stand in period dress in front of their New Freedom Hardware Store on West Main Street in August 1973.

Another item commemorating the centennial was this New Freedom license plate. It was bright yellow with blue lettering and was proudly displayed by many New Freedom residents during the centennial year and for years after. This particular plate is in a private collection of New Freedom memorabilia. It was never used and is in pristine condition.

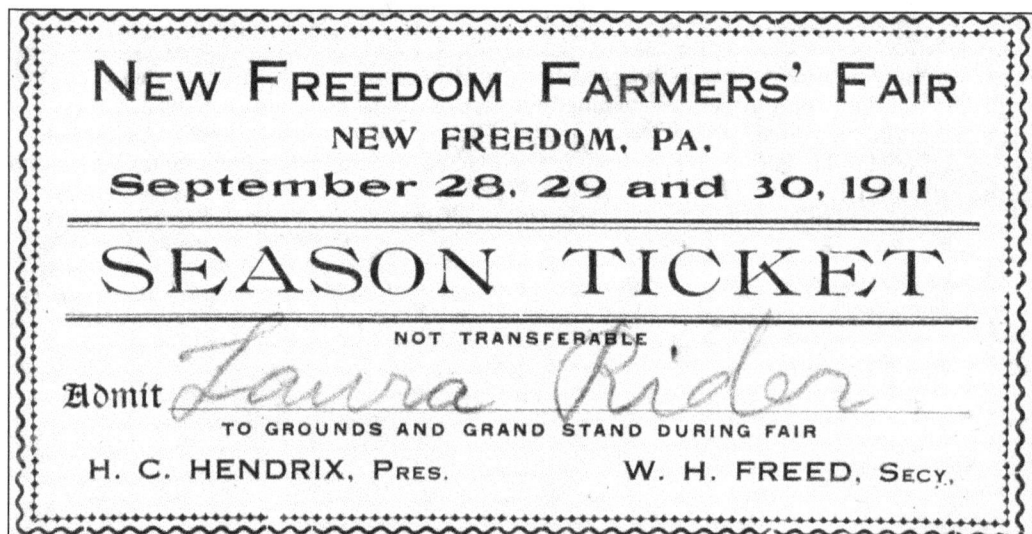

The New Freedom Farmers' Fair of the early 1900s can best be described as a combination of today's New Freedom Carnival and New Freedom Business Show. It was an annual fall event that was held on the land now occupied by the community center, Rose Fire Company, and Mervin Smith Woods. It provided an opportunity for local farmers and merchants to display their goods and an opportunity for the children of the community to enjoy games and other fun activities.

This late-1950s photograph shows the members and leaders of New Freedom Cub Scout Pack 24. Members are, from left to right, as follows: (first row) ? Baughman, unidentified, B. Smith, ? Harn, R. Amspacher, S. Bailey, and S. Myers; (second row) T. McCullough, R. Goodfellow, T. Corse, M. George, D. Bradfield, T. Berwager, F. Zeller, and D. Ratliff; (third row) S. Dickmeyer, J. Jones, S. Reed, E. Kiser, and G. Klinedinst; (fourth row) Almeda McCullough, Marge Goodfellow, Mary Reed, and Med Smith.

Like most towns in America, New Freedom has its share of model railroaders. One of the most desired and sought after modeling items is this HO-scale replica of the New Freedom train station. The kit consists of laser precision wooden pieces that are assembled with glue to make the 13-inch-long model of the station that was designed and built by the Pennsylvania Railroad in the mid-19th century.

This 1935 picture was taken beside 6 East Main Street (now Paesano Brothers') looking north across Main Street. The building in the background was part of the Bostic Restaurant and ice-cream business. Shown here are the following: (front row) "Ike" Wineholt (holding bike), Bob Mohar (on bike), Nelson Bostic (foot on wagon), Jesse Mays, Edward Sanderson (in wagon), Bob Franklin (football helmet) Donald Young (foot on wagon); (back row) "Buddy" Fletcher (coat and tie), "Buzz" Bostic (knit cap) and Ben Franklin (dress hat).

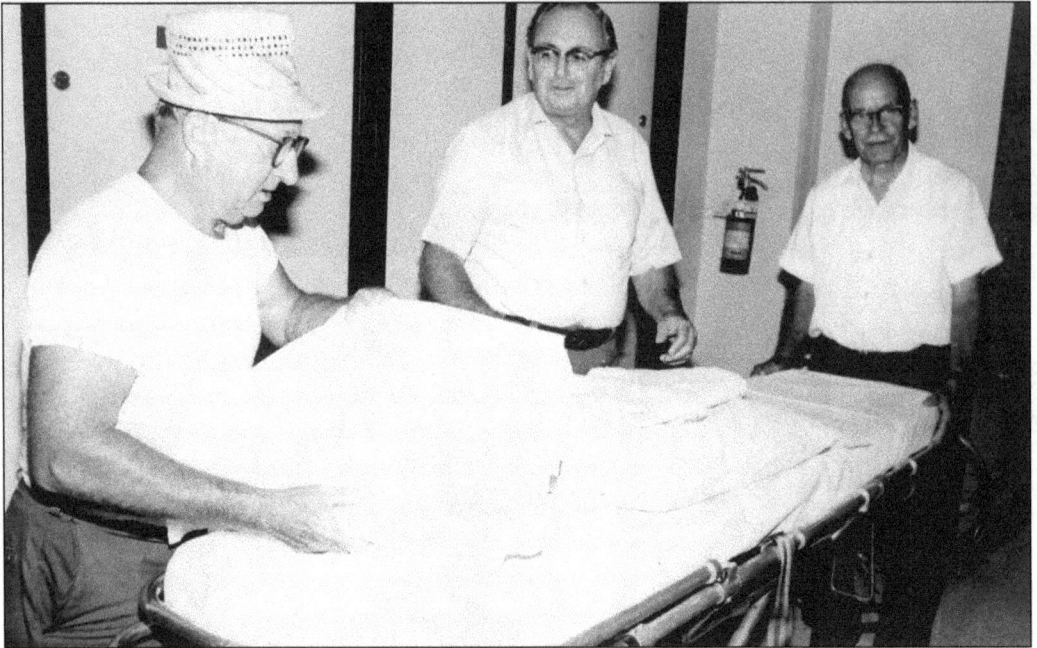

Like any small town, New Freedom thrived because of the many volunteers who pitched in to help others and to make the community a better place to live. Shown here are John Bailey (left), Wilbur Rehmeyer (center), and Mervin Smith, who volunteered their services in the summer of 1981 at the Memorial Osteopathic Hospital in York.

This large gathering of children from New Freedom is the 1925 Daily Vacation Bible School class. As it still does today, Daily Vacation Bible School consisted of music, games, crafts, and religious instruction for the children. As can be seen in this photograph, Vacation Bible School was once a community event, and nearly all of the town's children attended the single weeklong event. Today with the busy schedules of both adults and children, several churches hold Vacation Bible School at various times through the summer, and attendance is not nearly as good.

This patch was worn on the uniforms of New Freedom's police officers for many years. The design was different than the usual keystone shape used by the state police and numerous police and fire departments across the state. The emblem below was displayed on the borough police cars. At times during the department's history, officers used their own personal vehicles and attached the emblem by way of a magnetic backing. On January 1, 1992, New Freedom and Shrewsbury merged their police departments to form Southern Regional Police Department. In 1998, Glen Rock Borough joined the regional department.

NEW FREEDOM

HIGH SCHOOL

THIS CERTIFIES THAT

Daniel J. Mays

has satisfactorily completed the Course of Study prescribed by the Board of Education for the High School Department, and is therefore entitled to this

DIPLOMA

Given at New Freedom, Pennsylvania, this 28th *day of* May *A.D.* 1943

Henry S. Keith
SUPERVISING PRINCIPAL

Lloyd V. Bollinger
PRESIDENT BOARD OF EDUCATION

W. C. Bailey
SECRETARY BOARD OF EDUCATION

New Freedom Public School was built in the early 1900s. The school graduated a class every year between 1908 and 1951, except 1911, 1912, and 1914. New Freedom High School alumni meet annually in the town community center, which is the very building where they attended school. The event is attended by hundreds of graduates or former students of the school that served the New Freedom-Railroad-Shrewsbury area. Shown here is the diploma given to graduating students in 1943.

NEW FREEDOM HIGH SCHOOL

Hall-of-Fame

Daniel Jesse Mays

Class of 1943

THIS CERTIFIES THAT THE ABOVE NAMED HAS ACHIEVED INTERNATIONAL, NATIONAL OR LOCAL RECOGNITION BEYOND THE AVERAGE. HE OR SHE HAS ENHANCED THE ARTS AND SCIENCES: THE HUMANITIES AND INDUSTRY IN PARTICULAR AND HAS ENDOWED OUR "ALMA MATER" WITH HONOR AND ESTEEM. FOR THIS OUTSTANDING ACHIEVEMENT IN LIFE HE OR SHE HAS BEEN UNANIMOUSLY SELECTED BY THEIR PEERS TO BE ENSHRINED FOREVER IN THE NEW FREEDOM HIGH SCHOOL "HALL-OF-FAME."

ENSHRINED AT NEW FREEDOM, PENNSYLVANIA THIS 9th DAY OF May 19 92 BY: NEW FREEDOM HIGH SCHOOL ALUMNI ASSOCIATION.

Louise Alwine Winter '49
CHAIRMAN MEMBERSHIP COMMITTEE

Carroll L. Gemmill '49
CHAIRMAN N.F.H.S. ALUMNI REUNION

In 1983, the New Freedom High School Alumni Association established a hall of fame and began inducting members of each graduating class who distinguished themselves by achieving international, national, or local recognition beyond the average. The first induction ceremony included 26 members. To date, over 70 members have been so honored, including Hollywood actor Cameron Mitchell (class of 1937), professional baseball player and professional golfer Stewart C. Bowers Jr. (class of 1933), educator Claudia Bailey (class of 1924), judge Harvey Miller (class of 1909), portrait artist Dean Paules (class of 1949), pharmacist Leonard Itzoe (class of 1926), chemist Eugene Painter (class of 1929), educator and librarian Mary Crook (class of 1923), and professional baseball player Daniel Jesse Mays (class of 1943).

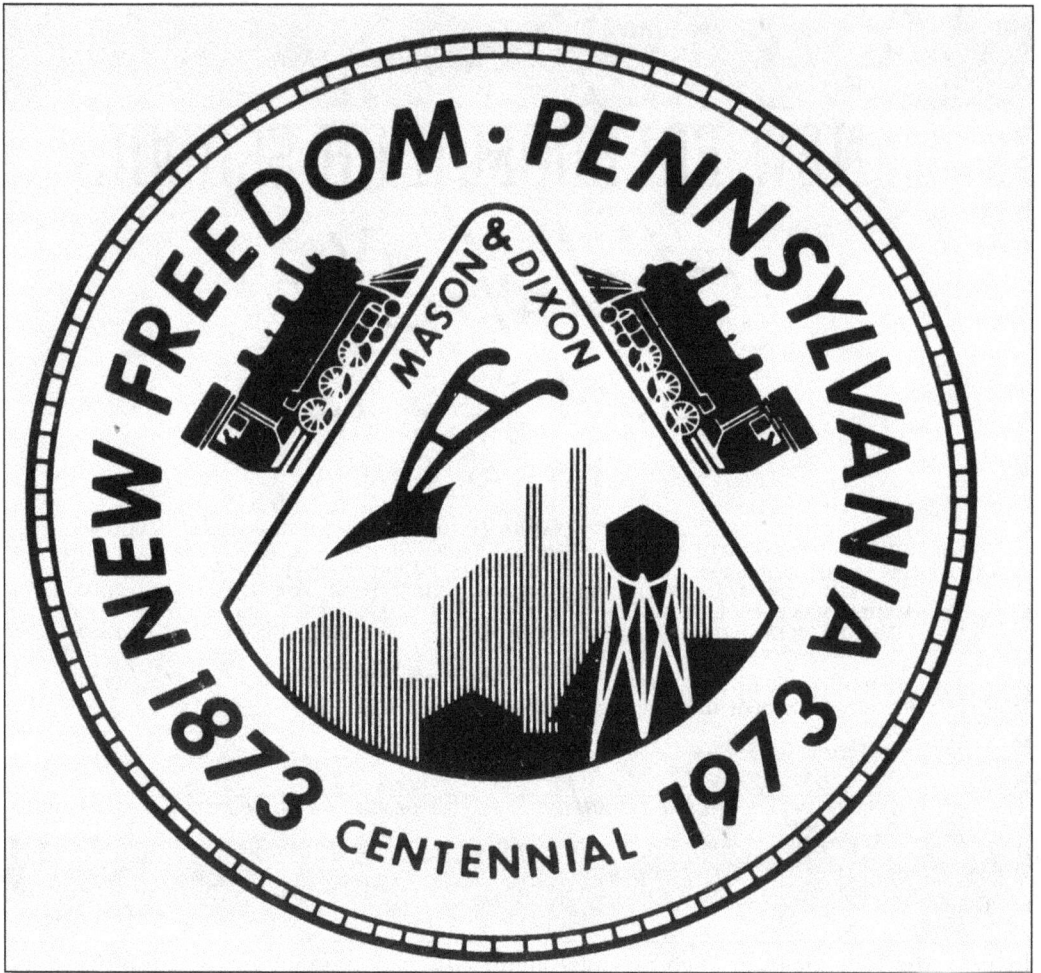

As this book goes to print, New Freedom is approaching its 132nd anniversary as an incorporated borough. It has survived the demise of a major railroad that, at one time, was its very lifeblood. The town has seen several large industries that provided a livelihood for its residents come and go. However, New Freedom continues to be one of the strongest and most close-knit communities in southern York County.